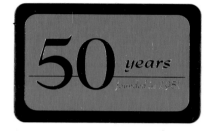

THE CITY

LIFE IN THE MIDDLE AGES

THE CITY

by Kathryn Hinds

BENCHMARK BOOKS

MARSHALL CAVENDISH
NEW YORK

With special thanks to Alexandra Service,
Ph.D., Medieval Studies, University of York, England,
for her assistance in reading the manuscript

The translations on pp. 49 (from *Le chevalier au lion,* by Chrétien de Troyes), 64 (from *The Canterbury Tales,* by Geoffrey Chaucer), and 61 ("The Boar's Head Carol," by anonymous) are by Kathryn Hinds. Population figures on p. 14 are from *Life in a Medieval City,* by Frances Gies and Joseph Gies. The recipes on p. 37 have been adapted from *The Medieval Kitchen: Recipes from France and Italy,* by Odile Redon et al., and *A Boke of Gode Cookery,* by James L. Matterer. The game on p. 57 has been adapted from *Medieval Holidays and Festivals: A Calendar of Celebrations,* by Madeleine Pelner Cosman. The descriptions on pp. 18 (government of Venice) and 44 (travels of Marco Polo) are adapted from *Venice and Its Merchant Empire,* by Kathryn Hinds.

Benchmark Books
Marshall Cavendish Corporation
99 White Plains Road, Tarrytown, New York 10591

Library of Congress Cataloging-in-Publication Data
Hinds, Kathryn (date)
Life in the Middle Ages: the City / by Kathryn Hinds
p. cm.
Includes bibliographical references and index.
Summary: Describes the development of cities during the late Middle Ages, A.D. 1100 through 1400,
discussing how they varied in government, commerce, population and culture and how they
influenced the shaping of European civilization.
ISBN 0-7614-1005-8 (lib.bdg.)
1. Civilization. Medieval—Juvenile literature. 2. Europe—Social life and customs—Juvenile literature.
3. Cities and towns—Europe—Juvenile literature. [1. Civilization, Medieval.
2. Cities and towns—Europe—History—to A.D.1500.] I. Title. II. Series.
CB351 .H52 2000 940.1—dc21 99-086689

Picture research by Rose Corbett Gordon, Mystic CT
Art Resource, NY: cover, 35, 68- The Pierpont Morgan Library; 10, 31- Giraudon; 12, 27, 42- Scala. *The Bodleian Library, University of Oxford:* 1- Ms Bodl.264 f.54v; 54- Ms Laud Misc.751 f.19v. *Bridgeman Art Library:* 2- Building of Marseilles from Histoire Universelle, c. 1286,Cott. Aug AV f.51v, British Library; 17- Painting by Antonio Pisanello, 1395-1455, Galleria dell'Accademia Carrara, Bergamo, Italy; 29- Celebration of Christmas Mass from 'Très Riches Heures du Duc de Berry', 1400-1416, by Limbourg Brothers, Musée Condé, Chantilly, France Roger-Viollet Paris; 41- From Livre des Symples Medichines, 15th c, Bibliothèque Nationale Paris; 43- Rustican, 15th c, by the Master of the Workshop of Margaret of York, Bruges, Bibliothèque Nationale Paris; 47- From Disocorides' 'De Herbis'(vellum), 15th c, France, Biblioteca Estense, Modena, Italy/Roger-Viollet Paris; 60- Chronique d'Angleterre from the Coronation of Richard II to 1387, 15th c, British Library; 64- British Library; 66- The Canterbury Tales Ellesmere Manuscript, Private Collection. *North Wind Pictures:* 19, 33, 38, 58. *Royal Library of Belgium, Brussels:* 21- Chronique de Hainaut, Ms 9242 f.274v. *Cliché Bibliothèque Nationale de France Paris:* 24, 26, 48, 55, 56. *Photothèque des Musées de la Ville de Paris:* 39. *Corbis:* 51- Archivo Iconographico SA; 62

Printed in Hong Kong
3   5   6   4   2

On the cover: Inside a merchant's house in Bruges, a city in present-day Belgium.
Painted around 1500 by Simon Bening.
On the half title page: Fairs and festivals in medieval cities featured many entertainments,
such as puppet shows like the one these children are enjoying.
On the title page: The building of the city of Marseilles, France, from a thirteenth-century manuscript.
Marseilles, founded by ancient Greek merchants, was one of the earliest cities in Europe.

TO DANAË

CONTENTS

ABOUT THE MIDDLE AGES

When we talk about the Middle Ages, we are talking about the period of European history from roughly 500 to 1500. Toward the end of this time, Italian writers and scholars known as humanists began to take a new interest in the literature and ideas of ancient Greece and Rome. The humanists wanted to create a renaissance, or rebirth, of ancient learning. They believed they were living in a new age, with a culture that was far superior to the culture of the previous ten centuries. So they called the years between the fall of Rome and their own time the Middle Ages, and the name has stuck.

The Italian humanists thought that the Middle Ages were dark, barbaric, ignorant, and without any kind of human progress. Today we often think of medieval times as a kind of storybook never-never land, with bold knights riding out on quests, jesters and wandering minstrels entertaining at sumptuous banquets, and kings and queens ruling from towered castles. But the real story about the Middle Ages is more fascinating than any fairy tale.

Just like life today, life in medieval times was full of complexity and variety. Very few people actually lived in castles; most were peasants who spent their lives farming in the countryside. However, as the Middle Ages progressed, cities steadily gained in importance. Old cities grew, and new cities were founded. The number of people living in cities greatly increased. These medieval city dwellers created great art, literature, and music. They worked at hundreds of crafts. They erected magnificent cathedrals that still stand. They had many of the same joys and sorrows, hopes and fears that we do, but their world was very different from ours.

Forget about telephones, newspapers, computers, cars, and televisions. Step back into time, to the years 1100–1400, the High Middle Ages. And let history come alive. . . .

A busy shop in a marketplace in medieval France

1

URBAN EUROPE

In ancient Greece and Rome, city life was well established. The Romans in particular developed an urban lifestyle, which they carried with them to every part of their empire. Everywhere from Britain to North Africa to Asia Minor there were thriving Roman cities.

After the collapse of the Roman Empire in 476, numerous cities fell into decay. Constant warfare brought trade—the lifeblood of cities—almost to a halt. In northwest Europe especially, rural life became far more important as power was concentrated in the hands of large landowners. Local farming was the most important element of the economy. Most areas produced only what they needed; there was rarely a surplus of food or goods that could be traded.

The Roman cities that survived—for example, Paris (France) and Cologne (Germany)—were often those where a bishop had his headquarters. A bishop was a high-ranking Christian priest who oversaw religious affairs for a particular region; a bishop's church was called a cathedral. But for some time even a cathedral city might be composed of only sixty to eighty small houses, and most of the city's area might still be gardens, orchards, and pastures.

At first the situation was better for cities in what is now

In this scene from the legend of Saint Ursula by artist Hans Memling, the saint and her companions arrive at the German city of Cologne. Cologne Cathedral, which rises in the background here, was begun in 1248. The city had started its life as a Roman colony twelve hundred years before that.

southern France, on the Mediterranean coast. Marseilles and other towns continued to do business with the ports of the eastern Mediterranean. This trade, too, was interrupted when Muslim warriors swept through the Mediterranean world in the seventh and eighth centuries. These warriors were fired with enthusiasm to spread the religion of Islam. Soon ancient cities such as Alexandria (Egypt) and Córdoba (Spain) again flourished, this time under Muslim rule. The followers of Islam also established thriving new cities, including Cairo (Egypt) and Baghdad (Iraq). During this period the only really great Christian city was Constantinople (now Istanbul, Turkey), center of the wealthy Byzantine Empire.*

Slowly, however, cities were beginning to make a comeback in northwest Europe. The sixth and seventh centuries saw the spread of Christian monasteries, highly organized communities devoted to religious life. Craftspeople, merchants, and farmers were quick to gather around the monasteries. Some of these monastic centers eventually grew into true cities, for example Germany's "Monks' Town"—Munich.

Trade was reviving, and market centers were starting to flourish. One such center was Dorestad in what is today the Netherlands. By the ninth century Dorestad and similar places were wealthy enough to attract Viking raiders. Many coastal and riverside settlements suffered heavily from Viking attacks. However, towns also strengthened their fortifications as a result of the Viking raids, and many fortresses built as defenses against the Vikings soon grew into cities. The Vikings themselves founded a number of new cities, and not only in their Scandinavian homeland: for example,

*The Byzantine Empire was the successor of the eastern half of the ancient Roman Empire. Its core was Asia Minor and Greece, and its culture was quite different from that of the rest of medieval Europe.

Dublin was one of many Irish cities established by the Vikings.

All of these upheavals had limited effect on northern Italy. Here, without interruption, city life continued to be of great importance. Milan, Florence, Pisa, Bologna, Verona, Padua, and Genoa had all been well-established urban communities since Roman times or even earlier. Rome itself, "the eternal city," maintained a special place in European culture, for its bishop, the pope, was the head of the Catholic Church of western Europe.

One major Italian city did not have its origin in the Roman Empire but actually arose during the Middle Ages. This was Venice,

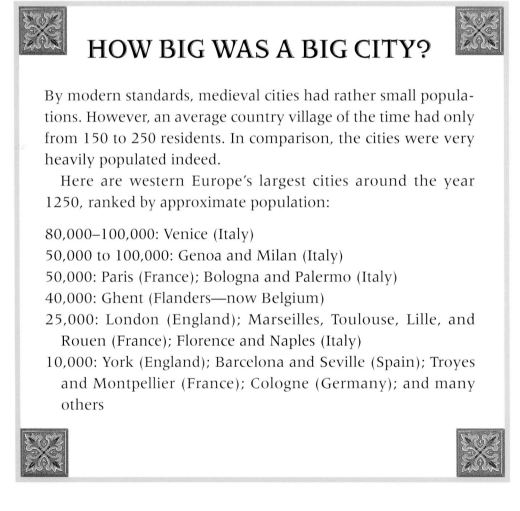

HOW BIG WAS A BIG CITY?

By modern standards, medieval cities had rather small populations. However, an average country village of the time had only from 150 to 250 residents. In comparison, the cities were very heavily populated indeed.

Here are western Europe's largest cities around the year 1250, ranked by approximate population:

80,000–100,000: Venice (Italy)
50,000 to 100,000: Genoa and Milan (Italy)
50,000: Paris (France); Bologna and Palermo (Italy)
40,000: Ghent (Flanders—now Belgium)
25,000: London (England); Marseilles, Toulouse, Lille, and Rouen (France); Florence and Naples (Italy)
10,000: York (England); Barcelona and Seville (Spain); Troyes and Montpellier (France); Cologne (Germany); and many others

founded in 697 by the union of several communities built on marshy islands just off the northeast coast of Italy. Within a few centuries Venice was a great power in the Mediterranean, and by 1201 it was the trading capital of Europe.

In northern Europe, the High Middle Ages saw the founding of other major cities, such as Belfast (Ireland), Amsterdam (Netherlands), Copenhagen (Denmark), and Berlin (Germany). Older cities continued to thrive and grow, making urban life a vital part of medieval culture.

2

WHO RAN THE CITIES?

There was no one standard type of government for medieval cities. Many were directly under royal control. For example, this was the case of Scandinavian towns such as Sigtuna, Sweden. Kings could profit a great deal from taxing trade goods that moved in and out of cities. When a town was under royal control, all fines from court cases went into the king's treasury. Often a king also received rents from numerous buildings in the cities under his rule. Furthermore, as kings increased their power over larger and larger areas, they found that cities were convenient centers from which to run the government. It was during the High Middle Ages that the idea of having a capital city took shape in Europe.

Royal control benefited townspeople, too. People who lived in a royal city were automatically free from serfdom: they were not required to work on a lord's land or pay the many fees that serfs owed their lords. In some parts of Europe, a serf could become free simply by moving to a city and living there for a year and a day.

A number of cities were under the rule of a count or other lord, who was usually a royal vassal. The French city of Troyes was ruled by the count of Champagne, a vassal of the king of France. The count received the same taxes, fines, and rents that royal cities paid to the king. Often both kings and counts encouraged trade and prosperity by guaranteeing protection for merchants traveling to the cities under their control.

In northern and central Italy it was not unusual for cities to have

Lionello d'Este, the duke of Ferrara, ran his city free of royal control.

GOVERNING A GREAT CITY: VENICE

The greatest medieval republic was the city of Venice. Its government evolved slowly over many centuries, taking its final form in the years from 1297 to 1310.

A duke, called the doge (DOHJ), was the head of state. His actual powers were quite limited, but he had great influence and prestige. His presence was required at every meeting of every branch of the government. Six dogal councillors assisted him and made certain that he did not try to increase his authority. These councillors were elected three at a time and stayed in office for only eight months. Together the doge, the dogal councillors, and the city's three chief judges fulfilled such duties as overseeing elections and making recommendations to the Senate.

The Senate was a body of 120 men elected for one-year terms, plus as many as 155 other officials. Some of these officials had the right to vote in the Senate, but some did not. The Senate dealt with foreign affairs, finances, trade policies, and other issues. It levied taxes and customs duties, declared war, and made the laws of the republic.

The senators and most other government officials were chosen by the Great Council. This council was made up of all Venetian noblemen aged twenty-five and above. Besides electing senators, judges, admirals, ambassadors, provincial governors, the doge, and others, the Great Council also debated political issues and approved the decisions of the Senate.

The members of the Great Council were under constant scrutiny by the Council of Ten. This group was formed in 1310 to protect the republic from enemies both outside and within. The ten councillors were elected for one-year terms by the Great Councillor. They saw that swift and ruthless punishment was dealt to any noble who abused his position, conspired to overthrow Venice's government, or plotted with foreign powers. The Council of Ten's authority was held in check by the Great Council, which could if necessary refuse to elect anyone to the Council of Ten.

The common people of Venice had little say in their government's decisions. However, during the Middle Ages they would gather in the city's main square to voice their approval or disapproval of the government's actions. The election of the doge also had to be ratified by the assembled people. Before a new doge took office, he was presented to the people with the words, "Here is your doge, if he is pleasing to you." This presentation gradually became a mere formality, although it continued to be greeted with cheers.

Venice, situated on a group of islands near the Adriatic Sea, was one of medieval Europe's most powerful cities. The great trading center was called the Queen of Cities.

nothing to do with royalty at all. Officially most of them were ruled by the Holy Roman Emperor. But in practice many were countries in their own right, sometimes themselves controlling other cities, along with rural areas.

These city-states were governed in various ways. For example, during the twelfth century many places hired a professional administrator, called a podestà, to run the city for a certain amount of time. Usually the podestà was from another region so that he could not be easily swayed by any of the different factions in the town he was overseeing. Other cities, such as Florence and Venice, were republics, where government officials were elected. During the thirteenth and fourteenth centuries some Italian city-states came to be ruled by independent dukes. These dukedoms usually became hereditary; for example, the dukes of Milan came from the Visconti family, and those of Ferrara from the Este family.

FREE CITIES

A striking feature of life in a large number of Italian cities was the commune, an institution that probably began in the eleventh century. A commune was a unified body that acted as the "voice" of the entire town. All the members of the commune were businessmen, who swore an oath of loyalty to one another and to the city. They pledged to defend their rights even against their lord. Members of the nobility and the clergy were usually not allowed to join the commune.

The Italian commune was imitated all over Europe. Numerous cities received charters of freedom from their lords, granting the right of self-government in return for an annual tax payment. In

The citizens of a city in Flanders (now Belgium) receive their charter of freedom.

England, where communes were known as boroughs, King John granted London the right to elect its own sheriff in 1199 and the right to elect its own mayor in 1215.

A number of bishops and other churchmen preached strongly against the communes, which they believed were destroying the social order. Many other lords seemed glad to see their subjects forming communes. A city that was a free commune attracted a great deal of business; the more business prospered, the more tax money the lord received.

Most free cities in northwest Europe were governed by a mayor and a town council. These officials served for set terms (the mayor of London's term of office was one year). At the end of this time they might choose their own successors. Alternatively, the new mayor and councilmen might be elected by a group of leading citizens, for instance the master craftsmen of the city. In all medieval European towns, the right to vote was limited to a relatively small number of people, usually the wealthiest men of the community. Even in a free city, there were many inequalities.

3
INSIDE THE CITY WALLS

he violence of the early Middle Ages taught town dwellers the importance of strong defenses. For this reason most towns were protected by tall, thick stone walls. Many cities kept growing after their walls were constructed. Often this meant that new buildings had to take the place of gardens and orchards inside the city walls. Sometimes a new wall had to be built to surround and protect the homes and businesses that had grown up outside the original wall. Only one major medieval city was not protected by walls: Venice, surrounded by water and possessing the strongest navy in Europe, needed no other defense.

A number of cities had not only walls but also a fortress or castle. In many cases the castle had been there first, and the city had grown up around it. The city of Edinburgh, for example, took shape along the road that led between the king of Scotland's castle and Holyrood Abbey. (An abbey was a large monastery or convent headed by an abbot or abbess.) Sometimes a city without a castle decided that it needed greater protection from enemies and built a new fortress for the purpose. In 1202 the king of France ordered the

A city in southern France nestles within its walls, while farm buildings, fields, and a monastery sprawl across the surrounding countryside.

building of a castle in Paris at a place by the Seine River where he thought the city's defenses were especially weak. The king himself did not live in the castle (he had a palace elsewhere in the city), but he did store his treasure there.

STREETS AND SQUARES

Visitors to a medieval city—perhaps attending a fair—entered through gates in the city's wall. (They might have to cross a drawbridge over a moat first.) Inside the wall they found streets lined with homes and businesses. Some buildings were painted red and blue or decorated in other ways. Signs with colorful pictures hung over the doorways of shops and taverns. Goods of all kinds were laid out on display on counters in front of the shops. Businesses of the same sort usually clustered together in the same part of the city or even on the same street. Visitors, as well as city residents, avoided the neighborhoods of the butchers and tanners as much as possible—these trades produced extremely unpleasant smells.

Streets were crowded with pedestrians, horses, and carts. Cats, dogs, geese, chickens, pigs, sheep, and cattle were also likely to be in the street. Many cities had at least two main thoroughfares, often running east to west and north to south. These tended to be fairly wide and straight. Other streets, however, usually were not. Some Paris streets were so narrow that only one person at a time could walk down them. Most streets in medieval cities were unpaved, muddy, foul, and smelly. In 1185 the king of France could no longer stand the odor coming from the mud, and he gave orders for the main streets of Paris to be paved with stones.

Throughout the medieval city were open squares, often in front of churches and generally unpaved. Sometimes a group of houses was built around a small square. Usually a city had at least one square large enough to serve as a gathering place for much of the population. Ten thousand or more people at a time could assemble in the square in front of Venice's Church of Saint Mark.

On the square in front of Notre Dame Cathedral in Paris, a pork market was held once a week. Most cities had various open-air markets, sometimes held in a church square and sometimes held in a district of the city dedicated to fairs and markets. Paris had a famous market called Les Halles, where the king had constructed

This fifteenth-century manuscript page shows tradesmen at work along a French city street. From left to right, there are tailors, furriers, a barber, and a grocer.

A busy market in fifteenth-century Italy. Most of the women merchants are keeping hold of their distaffs and spindles so that they can spin between sales.

two large buildings to shelter greengrocers, grain merchants, and dealers in small goods. Other towns also had permanent market buildings as well as open areas where visiting merchants could set up temporary stalls and tents.

GLORY TO GOD

Every neighborhood had its own parish church. Medieval churches were not only places of worship but also social centers. Meetings of various kinds, including town councils, were often held in churches. There was a church service every three hours, beginning at dawn. The ringing of the bells before each of these services marked the passage of time for city dwellers.

Many churches were dedicated to particular saints. The saints were people who had lived exceptionally holy lives and who had the power to perform miracles. Since God was often felt to be unreachable by ordinary humans, many Christians prayed to saints to "speak to" God in their behalf.

When seeking a saint's help, a person often prayed before a picture or statue of the saint or, if possible, at the saint's tomb or at a shrine to the saint. Some shrines housed relics—physical remains (usually bones)—of the saint. Holy relics had a great reputation for miraculous powers. During the Middle Ages people often traveled great distances on pilgrimages to visit churches that housed the relics of saints.

Some of the most splendid churches in medieval cities were the cathedrals. During the twelfth century a new style of architecture became very popular and was used for many cathedrals (as well as other churches). This style later came to be known as Gothic architecture. Recently developed engineering techniques allowed stone structures to soar to lofty heights. This was very effective in the new cathedrals, where tall, pointed arches and other features naturally drew worshipers' eyes up toward heaven.

The new style of building also allowed large windows to be set into the high walls of the cathedrals. Since colored glass was actually easier to produce at this time than perfectly clear glass, the church designers made a virtue of necessity and created stained glass windows. At first, pieces of glass were joined together in lead frames to make abstract designs. But very soon it was realized that pictures could be made with the colored glass. Stained glass windows illustrating episodes from the Bible and other religious scenes became an important feature of churches from then on. For many worshipers, who could neither read nor understand most of the

Gothic cathedrals, with their tall, pointed arches, splendid windows, and fine works of art, helped draw people's thoughts toward God.

church service (which was in Latin), these windows were their version of the Bible.

Probably the world's most famous Gothic cathedral is Notre Dame in Paris. Notre Dame, like many other Gothic cathedrals, took close to a century to complete. The work was done in stages, often halting for a time when money ran out. Yet no expense was spared in cathedral construction. Lords, prominent citizens, and groups of craftspeople all made donations to finance the new churches and their beautiful windows. These masterpieces in stone and glass not only glorified God but were also monuments to civic pride.

THE HALLS OF LEARNING

In addition to their other functions, cathedrals were centers of learning. Most had a cathedral school, originally organized by the bishop to educate future priests. In the eleventh century cathedral schools began to take additional students, sons of nobles, merchants, and other well-to-do citizens. By the twelfth century there were many renowned cathedral schools in Europe. Each school tended to have its own specialties, and students often traveled from school to school over the course of many years.

This was the beginning of the European university, a creation of the Middle Ages. By 1200 five great universities were taking form in the cities of Salerno and Bologna (Italy), Montpellier and Paris (France), and Oxford (England). By 1250 Europe boasted a total of twenty-two universities. Some were particularly noted for teaching law, others for medicine, and others for philosophy and religion.

University students might be as young as fourteen. For much of

A lecture at the University of Paris, around the year 1400. By this time university classes had become more formal than in earlier centuries. The professor teaches from a raised platform, while students sitting on benches take notes.

the Middle Ages they did not live in dormitories or study in libraries; universities at this time had few if any permanent buildings. Instead classes were held in the homes of professors, or even in rooms over taverns. Students sat on the floor, listening to lectures and debating

BROTHERS OF THE BRIDGE

The eleventh century saw the beginning of a wave of bridge building in western Europe. Ferries were becoming inadequate to deal with the increasing number of medieval travelers, especially merchants with their carts and trains of packhorses. Local lords, who profited from tolls collected at river crossings on their lands, realized that bridges could be a source of needed cash. The Church recognized bridges as a great help to travelers, especially pilgrims, and supported their construction.

In the twelfth century a group of devout men in southern France dedicated themselves to the good work of bridge building. These "Brothers of the Bridge" were responsible for the famous bridge of Avignon, which had a combination chapel and toll booth at one end. Even though the bridge became unusable in the 1600s, French children still sing and dance to an old folksong about it, "Sur le Pont d'Avignon" ("On the Bridge of Avignon").

Another medieval bridge later made famous in song was London Bridge. It was completed in 1209 and was the only bridge over the Thames River until 1750. Nineteen stone arches, each of them slightly different from the others, supported it. At one place in the bridge there was a gap covered by a drawbridge. If the city was ever attacked, this drawbridge could be raised to prevent enemies from crossing. Drawbridges had long been used over castle moats, but this is the first known use of the drawbridge at a river crossing.

As with bridges in other medieval towns, there were many houses and shops on London Bridge. A bridge was a good place to live and work, because water could easily be drawn from the river. Medieval city dwellers dumped their trash and sewage into the rivers, so waste disposal was also more convenient for people who lived on bridges. Unfortunately, this added to the unhealthiness of city living conditions in general.

London Bridge, with its many arches and houses, can be seen in the background of this view of the city in the late 1400s. In the foreground, King Henry VII sits in the White Tower, part of the Tower of London today.

points of logic, all in Latin. At night they returned to rented rooms to read or copy manuscripts by candlelight. After six years or so of study, they might take an examination and receive a license to teach. They might also become churchmen, lawyers, or doctors, or enter the service of a king or noble. No matter what career path a university student ended up choosing, one thing was certain: the pursuit of higher education was becoming a major element of city life, and of European culture in general.

4

HOME SWEET HOME

Most houses in medieval cities were built of wood, though some were of brick or stone. They could be up to four stories tall and were often narrow. As wooden houses aged, they tended to sag and lean. Sometimes they leaned so badly that the tops of houses on opposite sides of a street almost touched!

In poorer neighborhoods, several families lived in each house, renting their rooms from the house's owner. A very poor family might have only one room. This was often where they worked as well as where they cooked, ate, slept, and so on. If the father or mother was a weaver by trade, the loom probably took up most of the family's quarters.

In general, for city people their home was also their place of business. An independent craftsperson would have a shop and workshop on the ground floor of a house, and the family would live on the upper floors.

Wealthy merchants could have very large and splendid homes. In Venice, for example, such a house was usually three stories tall. The first level was given over to business. The front entrance, facing the water, had a quay or dock. (Venice had canals instead of streets, boats and ships instead of carts and trains of packhorses.) The central doorway led into a spacious hall where goods could be unloaded,

This painting by Simon Bening shows the inside of a wealthy merchant's home in Flanders around 1500.

counted, and inspected. On either side of this, and half its height, were storerooms. The merchant had his offices on an in-between level above the storerooms. On the second floor was a large central hall that was often used as a showroom for merchandise. It was also the place where banquets, weddings, and other gatherings were held. To the sides of this hall were the family's living quarters. The top floor provided rooms for servants and employees.

ALL THE COMFORTS OF HOME?

Even for wealthy families, living conditions were not what we would think of as comfortable. Fireplaces were the only source of heat and often the main source of light. Oiled parchment was the most common window covering, and windows were usually small and narrow to begin with. Oil lamps and smoky tallow candles tended to be lit only after dark.

The main room of a private house, sometimes called the solar, was where the family dined. It contained benches, one or two cupboards for storing dishes and utensils, and a trestle table (which was only set up at mealtimes). In well-to-do homes, panels of dyed or embroidered cloth hung on the walls. Beginning in the early 1300s, tapestries—more elaborate wall hangings—became available to the wealthy. At this time, too, rugs began to be common in European cities; before this floors were usually covered only with rushes, sometimes with fragrant herbs and flowers added.

The kitchen was often behind the solar. The kitchen's main feature was a huge fireplace, where all the cooking was done. There was a long worktable, a large vat for water, and a spice cabinet. Of

SPICE IT UP!

In the Middle Ages spices were a luxury. Merchants who traded in spices could make huge profits. These merchants and other well-to-do city dwellers enjoyed highly spiced food. From near Venice comes a recipe for a spice mixture that could be used "for all foods": one part black pepper, one part cinnamon, one part ginger, one-quarter part saffron, and one-eighth part cloves.

Another spicy medieval recipe, this time from England, is for a kind of ginger candy: Boil a quart of honey, and skim off any scum that rises to the top. Remove from heat and add a pinch of saffron, a pinch of white pepper, and a few pinches each of ginger and cinnamon. Thoroughly stir in plain, white bread-crumbs—enough to make the honey a very thick mass. Let the mixture cool slightly, then pour it out onto a flat surface and pat it into a square or rectangle. When it is cooled completely, cut it into small squares, stick a whole clove into each square, and enjoy!

course the kitchen also contained pots, cauldrons, trivets, mortars and pestles, spoons, and a number of other cooking utensils. Many houses had small gardens to supply the kitchen with herbs and vegetables.

The great writer Christine de Pisan (1363–1430), daughter of a doctor from Venice, presents a copy of one of her books to the queen of France. The queen's richly canopied bed is similar to the beds in which wealthy townspeople slept.

Bedroom furniture included a washstand, a chest, and perhaps a table and a few chairs. Adults slept in huge canopied beds; children's beds were smaller and plainer. There were no closets for clothes. Garments were stored in chests or hung up on hooks on the wall or on a rod behind the bed. People slept naked or in their underclothes.

Cleanliness was a challenge in the medieval city. Water for drinking, cooking, and washing had to be carried from a well outside the house; often many houses shared a single well. People generally bathed once a week at most. Fleas, bedbugs, and lice were constant problems. To go to the bathroom, most people had to use an outhouse in the yard. At night, they could use a chamber pot that was kept under the bed. Some homes might have a garderobe, a kind of indoor outhouse, off the bedroom. Garderobes often emptied into nearby canals, streams, or ditches, contributing to the city's smelly and unhealthy atmosphere.

It was hard to keep clean in the Middle Ages. Hair lice were a common problem. Here a man gets a thorough scrubbing.

5

CITY FOLKS

With the growth of cities in the Middle Ages, a new class of people became increasingly important in European society. These people were not rulers or nobles with large landholdings, and they were not peasant farmers or common laborers. They were a middle class: merchants, bankers, doctors, lawyers, and skilled craftspeople. Middle-class property owners and master craftsmen—called bourgeois, burghers, burgesses, or similar names in much of northwest Europe—were a town's leading citizens. They paid a share of the borough's annual tax to the king and enjoyed a number of privileges in return, including the rights to vote and hold city offices.

Although burghers were highly influential, their numbers were relatively small. Most city residents were common working people with no say in how the city was run. Many of these people lived comfortably enough, but others were very poor. Some were unable to make a regular living and resorted to begging. This became a greater problem as increasing numbers of peasants left the countryside in the hope of gaining freedom and finding more profitable work in the towns.*

*To learn more about the peasants, see *The Countryside*, another title in this series.

 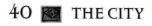

Merchants such as these jewelers were part of the middle class that became so important in medieval cities. In addition to jewelry and objects plated with silver or gold, this shop sells precious stones. In the Middle Ages gemstones not only were valued for their beauty, but were also believed to have the power of curing or preventing various illnesses.

Hospitals began to appear in a number of medieval cities. These hospitals were usually established by the Church and run by monks and sometimes nuns. They not only treated sick people but also fed and clothed the poor. Some hospitals also provided food and shelter for pilgrims, and others cared for orphans. Saint Catherine's Hospital in Paris gave free lodging to poor widows and young girls who came to the city looking for work. By 1180 Paris also had three colleges, which provided cheap housing for impoverished university students.

Doctors and patients in an Italian hospital

URBAN MELTING POTS

Medieval cities were meeting places for people of many nationalities. A city where the king held court would be visited from time to time by foreign ambassadors. If a city had a university, it attracted students from all over Europe. Pilgrims, too, journeyed to cities in a number of different countries. Other visitors or temporary residents

Stone masons and carpenters build a medieval church.

in towns were traveling preachers and wandering entertainers.

Cities that were erecting new churches and cathedrals "imported" many of the skilled craftspeople needed for the construction. These workers, from a variety of places, often lived in temporary housing right in the cathedral yard. Master masons, master carpenters, bell founders, and window makers in particular traveled from building site to building site as their services were needed.

MARCO POLO

The most famous of all medieval merchants was Marco Polo. In 1271, at the age of seventeen, Marco Polo left Venice with his father and uncle. They were heading for China, which the two older men had already visited once. After a four-year journey the Polos reached China's eastern coast and the court of the emperor, Kublai Khan.

The emperor was extremely impressed with Marco Polo's abilities and took the young Venetian into his service. Over the course of the next seventeen years Marco was given numerous diplomatic missions, which took him not only all over China but also to India, Persia, Tibet, Burma (today's Myanmar), and Vietnam. Everywhere he went, he carefully observed and remembered scenery, people's customs, and details of local trade.

At last the Polos grew homesick, and in 1292 they set out for Venice. Arriving home after an arduous journey over land and sea, they were greeted with astonishment and disbelief. The tales they told of their travels and their long stay in the East were incredible. But the rich robes and fabulous jewels they brought back, proof of the wealth of the East, made a deep impression on their fellow Venetians.

As for Marco, he eventually turned the story of his adventures into a book. *The Travels of Marco Polo* became a medieval best-seller. Aside from describing the wonders of the East, Marco's book provided extremely accurate geographical information. For centuries his book was referred to by mapmakers and explorers, including Christopher Columbus.

Marco Polo died in 1324. It is said that his last words were, "I did not write half of what I saw."

Trade was the force that brought the most visitors of all into the medieval city. The great fairs held twice a year in the French city of Troyes attracted merchants not only from all of France but also from Spain, Italy, Germany, Flanders, England, Scotland, and Scandinavia. Venice had so many foreign merchants visiting on a regular basis that in the early 1300s the city began to construct permanent business centers for them. Venetian merchants themselves voyaged to most of the known world, everywhere from England to North Africa to Constantinople and beyond. Many Venetians and others lived and did business in foreign cities for years at a time.

Medieval cities commonly had large Jewish populations. Church law prohibited Jews from owning land and from earning their living by manufacturing or selling goods to the general public. At the same time Christians were generally forbidden to make loans and charge interest. Jews were therefore able to play an important role as bankers and moneylenders in many cities.

City governments were often tolerant of Jews, especially when this proved profitable. But all too often during the Middle Ages, a ruler needing money would expel the Jews from the area under his rule, confiscating all of their property and belongings. This happened in Paris in 1182. Sixteen years later the banished Jews were allowed to return to the city, but only after paying a tax to the king.

Even worse, Jews were sometimes targets of extreme violence. For example, in 1190, 150 Jewish men, women, and children were killed in the city of York, England. Even in the international atmosphere of the medieval city, the Christian majority had difficulty understanding and accepting religious differences.

6

TAKING CARE OF BUSINESS

Medieval cities were not only centers of commerce, they were also centers of manufacturing. Some cities specialized in particular products. Many towns of Flanders were noted for their woolen cloth; the Italian city of Lucca specialized in silk cloth. Milan, Italy, was a source of armor, crossbows, and other military equipment. Venice was famous for its glass, used for windows, mirrors, goblets, beads, and more.

The citizens of a prosperous medieval town might work at more than a hundred different crafts and trades. In a large city like Paris the number of different occupations could be close to two hundred. Many trades were family affairs, with husband, wife, and children all sharing in the work. Sometimes husband and wife worked at two different trades, however. Widows and single women often supported themselves (and sometimes their children, too) through crafts or various businesses.

In much of Europe during the High Middle Ages, women worked at almost as many kinds of jobs as men did. Only a few professions were totally closed to women at this time: they could not be sailors, notaries, lawyers, or priests. But we have records from around

1300 that tell of women—especially in France, Germany, and England—who were merchants, money changers, jewelers, goldsmiths, artists, stone masons, entertainers, tavern keepers, shoemakers,

Glassblowers at work in the fifteenth century

A blacksmith at her forge

leather workers, shield makers, archers, gatekeepers, millers, black-
smiths, brewers, wine dealers, food sellers, fishmongers, bakers, ped-
dlers, dyers, yarn makers, wool weavers, linen workers, tailors,
dressmakers, hat makers, furriers, hairdressers, candle makers, spice
dealers, pharmacists, doctors, surgeons, and barbers (who not only
cut hair but also performed minor surgery and set broken bones). As
household servants, laundresses, nurses, wax dealers, silk spinners,
silk weavers, embroiderers, and lace makers, Parisian women out-
numbered men in 1292. Unfortunately, as in so many other times

THE COMPLAINT OF THE WOMEN SILK WEAVERS

Chrétien de Troyes (1135–1190) was one of the most popular writers in medieval France. He wrote several long poems that told stories about King Arthur and the knights and ladies of his court. Chrétien was a city dweller, though, and even in his courtly tales he included vivid descriptions of urban life. The following selection, translated from his *Yvain, or The Knight of the Lion*, vividly portrays the difficult working and living conditions of many townspeople:

> *Always we weave the silken cloth;*
> *Never are we ourselves well clothed.*
> *Always we are poor and in distress,*
> *And always we suffer hunger and thirst,*
> *Never knowing what it is to succeed*
> *Or even to have enough to eat:*
> *In the morning we share a little bread,*
> *And in the evening even less.*
>
> . . .
>
> *We are so poor, we barely live,*
> *While that man for whom we slave*
> *Enriches himself from our plight.*
> *We stay awake a great part of the night*
> *And all the day making money for him,*
> *For he threatens to break our limbs*
> *If we rest even with good cause,*
> *And so we dare not stop or pause.*

and places, medieval women routinely earned less money than men, even for the same work.

Women who didn't work for pay still worked hard, raising children and keeping house. Even with a servant or two to help, household chores were time consuming and often demanded a great deal of strength from the medieval housewife. Only women in very wealthy families avoided physical labor completely.

GUILDS

During the Middle Ages people who worked at the same craft or trade typically belonged to a guild. Guilds set standards for products and workmanship, regulated wages and employment practices, paid for members' funerals, and looked after members' interests in other ways.

Around 1300, Paris had five guilds whose members were all women; Cologne (Germany) had four. (In both cities, these women-only guilds were primarily dedicated to various stages in the making of silk cloth.) There were many guilds in a number of cities where women were very active in their own right, even though most members were male. In other guilds, women could not be admitted unless they were wives, widows, or, sometimes, daughters of male guild members. It seems that virtually the only guilds that were completely closed to women throughout Europe were the guilds of the great merchants.

One of the guild's most important functions was to regulate the training of apprentices, or student craftspeople. Depending on the difficulty of the craft, an apprentice spent from four to twelve years learning his or her trade from a master. During this time the

*An apprentice alchemist stirs his brew while his master reads the "recipe."
Alchemists were medieval chemists who believed they could find a recipe for
turning base metals into gold.*

apprentice usually lived in the master's home, and the master sup-
plied the apprentice with food and clothing as well as training. The
apprentice not only learned from but also assisted the master, even
helping out with household chores when necessary.

When apprentices finished their training, they had to prove
to the guild that they knew their craft or trade, and they had to
show that they had the money or tools to go into business for themselves. They swore that they were loyal and careful and that they
would practice their profession honestly and responsibly. Finally,
after paying a fee, they were accepted as masters and full members
of their guild.

HARD WORK

Not all workers in medieval cities belonged to guilds. Some trades did not have guilds. Some people worked at their craft, even training apprentices, without ever belonging to the guild for it. But most city dwellers did not have specialized, skilled crafts or trades. Unskilled laborers probably made up the majority of workers in the medieval city. Often they had no regular employment, but took whatever jobs were available, day by day. In addition, many townspeople were involved in agriculture. Every morning they left the city to work in fields, orchards, vineyards, or pastures outside the city walls. They returned to their urban homes before watchmen or guards closed the city gates for the night.

However they earned their living, most people in medieval cities worked very hard. The average workday was from ten to fourteen hours long. Unless there was a holiday during the week, Sunday was the only day off—and, as many preachers complained, large numbers of people preferred to rest and relax on Sunday rather than attend church.

7

GROWING UP IN A MEDIEVAL CITY

In the Middle Ages all babies were born at home. During labor, a city woman was often assisted by a midwife. She was also visited and encouraged by various female relatives, friends, and neighbors. (No men were allowed to be present.) In a well-to-do household, dishes of candied fruits and nuts were put out for the benefit of these visitors, and some of the family's best possessions were displayed in the woman's room.

Even in wealthy families, childbirth was difficult and dangerous. No one at this time knew about the risk of infection or about ways to prevent it. If something went wrong while a woman was giving birth, there was little the midwife could do. Sometimes she would whisper magical chants into the mother's ears, even though the Church disapproved of such things. Many babies and mothers died during or soon after birth.

If everything went well, the midwife immediately washed the newborn baby and then wrapped it securely in swaddling bands. (These bands were tight enough to keep the baby from moving, for fear that too much movement would cause its arms and legs to

This painting from a fifteenth-century manuscript shows a midwife drying off a newborn baby before placing him in his mother's arms.

twist out of shape.) Then the baby was shown to its father for the first time.

Soon afterward, in a Christian family, the baby was taken to church to be baptized. A female relative carried the child, followed by the father, the godparents, the midwife, and various friends and family members; the mother, however, remained at home. During the ceremony a priest anointed the baby with oil and dipped him or her into holy water. The godparents assisted, giving their promise to see that the child was raised according to the teachings of the Church. Townspeople often liked to choose rich and important citizens to be their children's godparents.

Back at home, the newborn was placed in a wooden cradle at its mother's bedside. Nearly all medieval babies were breast-fed, but well-to-do city dwellers generally hired a servant, called a nurse, for this purpose. The nurse fed and bathed the baby every three hours.

A mother rocks her baby in its cradle. The five-pointed star carved at the foot of the cradle was a powerful symbol of protection during the Middle Ages.

CHILDHOOD

When babies were old enough to sit up, they were released from their swaddling. From then on they wore adult-style clothes. About half of all children died before they reached the age of five. Those who lived spent their early years mostly in play. Children in well-off families might have tops, wooden swords, hobby horses, stilts, marbles, dolls made out of wood or clay, and similar toys. Other children had to use their imaginations and whatever they could find—sticks, leaves, flowers, horseshoes, blocks of wood, and even bread crusts. Many children had fun with balloons made from the bladders of recently slaughtered pigs. Like adults, children might enjoy games such as chess, checkers, backgammon, dice games, lawn bowling, wrestling, and blindman's bluff.

A group of boys enjoy a game known as frog-in-the-middle.

 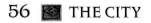

HUNT THE SLIPPER
A MEDIEVAL GAME

This game was enjoyed by both children and adults in medieval towns and cities, where cobbling (repairing shoes) was a common trade.

To play hunt the slipper, the players need to sit in a tight circle on the floor or in chairs. One player, called Slipper Soul, sits or stands in the middle of the circle. She or he should be holding a slipper or shoe. While the other players pretend to be cobblers hard at work, Slipper Soul says:

> *Cobbler, cobbler,*
> *Mend my shoe!*
> *Make it all anew.*
> *Three stitches will do!*

With that, Slipper Soul hands the shoe or slipper to one of the players in the circle, then closes his or her eyes for several seconds. The other players pass the shoe from one to another behind their backs. When Slipper Soul's eyes are open again, everyone continues to pretend that they are passing the shoe around the circle. Slipper Soul must guess who actually has it. When that person is identified, he or she takes the shoe into the middle of the circle, becoming the next Slipper Soul, and the game begins all over again!

Boys attending grammar school in the mid-fourteenth century

Around the age of seven children began to prepare for their adult roles. Some boys and girls in medieval cities attended grammar school, where they learned basic arithmetic and reading. Boys could go on to more advanced studies at a cathedral school, and then perhaps at a university. For girls, the rest of their education usually took place at home and focused on cooking, cloth making, and other skills needed to run a household and care for a family. However, a number of girls as well as boys began an apprenticeship sometime between the ages of seven and twelve. Many others went straight to work, doing whatever was necessary to assist their parents.

Childhood was short, but so was life. Most girls married when they were teenagers and were soon raising children of their own. After only ten or fifteen years of marriage, they might well find themselves widows, for husbands were typically ten, twenty, or thirty years older than their wives. During the Middle Ages fifty was considered a ripe old age.

8

FEAST DAYS AND PLAYS

C ity life was not all work and no play. There were many holidays throughout the year when everyday work ceased. Most of these holidays were Christian feast days, although sometimes the celebrations did not seem very religious. Venice celebrated the Feast of the Purification of the Virgin Mary (February 2) with boat races on the city's Grand Canal. On the Feast of the Holy Innocents (December 28) French choirboys switched places with cathedral officials and conducted the church services. Another holiday saw low-ranking priests wearing their robes inside out, nibbling sausages in church, and braying like donkeys during the worship service!

As with Christians today the most important holidays were Christmas and Easter. Before each there was a period of many weeks when people were supposed to turn their thoughts away from worldly pleasures, spend extra time in prayer, and purify themselves of sin as much as possible. When Christmas and Easter finally arrived, everyone celebrated as lavishly as they could afford to. Wealthy families had elaborate feasts, serving up to ten courses.

As minstrels play and servants offer platters of food, a group of fourteenth-century noblemen enjoy an elaborate feast.

Such feasts often included entertainment by musicians, singers, jugglers, and acrobats.

Plays were another favorite holiday entertainment in medieval cities. In the church services for Christmas and Easter, priests often acted out parts of the Bible stories of Jesus' birth and resurrection. These mini-plays were all in Latin, but they were so popular with worshipers that longer plays were eventually presented in French, German, and English. By the thirteenth century Christmas and Easter plays were being given outdoors in front of the church. The plays portrayed episodes from the Bible, such as the story of Adam and Eve, as well as stories of the lives and miracles of various saints.

THE BOAR'S HEAD CAROL
A SONG FROM MEDIEVAL ENGLAND

The words of this carol were first written down in the 1400s at the University of Oxford. Students and professors probably sang it as a procession brought in the main dish of the Christmas feast, a boar's head bedecked with garlands of greenery. Versions of "The Boar's Head Carol" are sometimes still sung at Christmastime today.

Before me I bear the head,*
Singing praises to the Lord.

The boar's head in hands I bring,
With garlands gay and birds singing.
I pray you all to help me sing,
You here at this gathering.

Before me I bear the head,
Singing praises to the Lord.

The boar's head, I understand,
Is the chief dish served in all this land.
And everywhere it may be found,
It is served with good mustard.

Before me I bear the head,
Singing praises to the Lord.

The boar's head, I dare well say,
Soon after Yuletide's twelfth day,
He takes his leave and goes away—
Then he has left our country.

Before me I bear the head,
Singing praises to the Lord.

*Words in italics were originally in Latin.

In the English city of York, players enact the biblical story of the Sacrifice of Abraham. Nobles watch the procession from a platform elevated above the crowded square.

Comedy was combined with serious religious lessons so that the watchers would stay interested.

A number of English towns gradually developed cycles of plays that dramatized all the major events in the Bible, from the Creation to the Last Judgment. These play cycles came to be presented in squares and marketplaces around the feast of Corpus Christi (fifty-four days after Easter), which was celebrated with splendid processions through the city streets. Each individual play was produced by a specific guild, with guild members acting all the parts. In these English towns and in other medieval European cities, theater was evolving into the art form we know today.

CHAUCER'S URBAN PILGRIMS

Geoffrey Chaucer, a resident of London, was one of the greatest writers in English literature. He was born around 1340 and died in 1400. His most famous book is *The Canterbury Tales*, in which a group of people on a pilgrimage to the Shrine of Saint Thomas à Becket in Canterbury entertain one another by telling stories. Several of the pilgrims are typical city dwellers; among them are the Merchant, the Clerk, the Five Guildsmen, and the Wife of Bath. Here, adapted into modern English, are Chaucer's descriptions of these urban travelers:

THE MERCHANT

A merchant was there with a forked beard;
Richly clothed, high on his horse he sat.
On his head was an imported beaver-fur hat.
His boots were buckled most carefully.
He spoke his views very solemnly,
Always looking to the increase of his earnings.
He wished the sea kept safe more than anything.
. . .
This worthy man could use his head,
And no one knew if he was in debt,
So discreetly did he do his business,
With bargains and with making loans.

THE CLERK

A clerk from Oxford was there also,
Who began to study logic long ago.

A portrait of Geoffrey Chaucer

His horse was just as thin as a rake;
And he was not right fat, I undertake,
But looked hollow and full of care.
His outer cloak was all threadbare.
. . .
He would rather have by the head of his bed
Twenty books, bound in black or red,
Of Aristotle and his philosophy,
Than rich robes or music to make merry.
For all that he was a philosopher,
He had very little gold in his coffer;
But all he received that his friends lent,
On books and on learning it was spent,
And he would pray for the souls' ease
Of those who gave to him for his studies.
In thinking he took most care and most heed.
He spoke not one word more than he'd need,
And that was said in proper form and reverence,
And short and sweet, full of deep significance.
Full of moral virtue was his speech;
And gladly would he learn, and gladly teach.

THE FIVE GUILDSMEN

A haberdasher and a carpenter,
A weaver, a dyer, and a rug maker—
They all wore the badge and garb bestowed
On members of a tradesmen's brotherhood.
. . .
Each of them seemed a fair burgess
To sit in a guildhall on the dais.
Every one, on account of his wisdom,
Was well suited to be a councilman.
As for property and income, they had plenty—
And with this their wives would well agree,

Or else they were certain to complain;
It is very pleasant to be called "Madame,"
To walk at the head of holy-day processions,
And to wear a cloak as fine as a queen's!

THE WIFE OF BATH

From a suburb of Bath a good wife came,
But she was somewhat deaf, and that was a shame.
For making cloth she had such a bent,
She surpassed the famous weavers of Ghent.

. . .

Her many kerchiefs were finely textured—
I daresay that when she went to church,
They weighed ten pounds upon her head!
Her hose were of fine scarlet red,
Tightly tied, and her shoes were soft and new.
Bold was her face, and fair, and red of hue.
She was a worthy woman all her life.
As for husbands, she'd had five.

. . .

Three times she'd been to Jerusalem.
She had passed many a strange stream—
She had been to Rome and to Bologne,
To Saint James's shrine and to Cologne.

. . .

On an ambling horse she easily sat,
Bundled up well, on her head a hat
As wide around as a knight's shield,
A warm outer skirt from her hips to her heels.
On her feet she wore a pair of sharp spurs.
She laughed and joked with all the travelers.

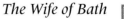

The Wife of Bath

9

DISASTERS AND DISEASE

Today many people think of cities as dangerous places to live because of crime. There was crime in medieval cities, too, but there were also many more dangers from natural disasters, fire, warfare, and disease.

Most medieval towns were built next to rivers or the sea, and so flooding was a constant threat. In 1197 a terrible flood struck Paris, swamping the bridges and wiping out whole neighborhoods. The city suffered almost equally bad floods in 1206, 1220, and 1221. Towns in the Netherlands were flooded repeatedly; one thirteenth-century flood killed more than fifty thousand people living near the Dutch coast.

Fire was a huge danger in all medieval cities, for most urban buildings were built of wood and were crowded together. It took only one tipped-over candle or one spark from a fireplace to start a blaze that could destroy an entire neighborhood. When fire broke out, there were no professional firefighters to call on. Hastily organized bucket brigades were usually not enough to combat spreading flames.

Another constant threat was warfare. Italian city-states were frequently at war with one another. Other cities suffered in the

conflicts between nations, such as the Hundred Years' War between England and France. City walls were usually strong enough to resist attackers—unless the attackers were able to tunnel under the wall. However, if an enemy laid siege to the city, the residents did not have enough food to hold out indefinitely. Even in times of peace, it could be difficult to ensure a constant food supply for medieval towns. And where there was war and hunger, diseases always followed.

THE BLACK DEATH

The worst disease of the Middle Ages was the Black Death. This fearful plague swept through western Europe repeatedly during the fourteenth through the seventeenth centuries. The first wave of the disease, from 1347 to 1350, was the most devastating. Nearly every European city lost from one quarter to two thirds of its population. One chronicler recorded that from May to September 1348, 96,000 people died in Florence alone. Whole families were wiped out. There was no cure, and almost everyone who came down with the plague died from it, usually within four days.

Many city dwellers fled to the countryside, hoping to escape the dreaded disease. There was no escape; the Black Death struck rural villages and country mansions, too. By the time the epidemic ended, western Europe had lost roughly half its population.

Christian Europeans tried to understand why God had

People in the Middle Ages were never free from the threat of war. In this manuscript painting, made in the twelfth century, Danes attack an English town.

allowed such a terrible disease to suddenly kill so many. Sometimes they blamed foreigners or other "strangers" for bringing the plague to their city or country. The result was increased suspicion—and often persecution—of outsiders such as Jews and lepers (people who were already outcasts because they suffered from leprosy, a very serious skin disease).

The plague had other far-ranging effects on European society. Business and trade had come to a complete halt during the epidemic. When it was over, the economy had to be totally rebuilt. Labor was scarce and prices were high. Peasants and laborers demanded more rights and higher wages. Because of the scarcity and cost of labor, the Church permitted Christians to own non-Christian slaves. Governments passed laws that preserved the privileges of the upper class. Guilds tightened their rules, seeking to protect their members from competition, especially competition from women and others who would work for low wages.

After 1350 guilds and governments placed increasing limits on the work that women could do. For example, women were banned from being doctors, on the grounds that they could not receive a university medical license. (They were not allowed to attend universities at all.) Some women continued to work as doctors—often with great success—but they were frequently arrested, tried, and fined for practicing medicine without a license. Women were banned from many crafts, too, and admitted to fewer and fewer guilds. Not until the twentieth century would large numbers of women again enjoy the opportunity to work at the great variety of trades they had enjoyed in the city of the High Middle Ages.

Europe's towns did make some strides forward following the Black Death of 1347–1350. Public health became a new area of government concern as cities explored various measures to keep diseases from spreading. City governments, at least in northern Italy, had long been concerned with controlling pollution. Their efforts in this area increased, and there were efforts to improve sanitation as well.

Some towns never fully recovered from the disasters of the fourteenth century. Many others, however, went on to grow and thrive, continuing as centers of education, culture, and commerce. We can look to these medieval towns as the forerunners of the cities of today.

GLOSSARY

bishop   a high-ranking Catholic priest who oversees religious affairs for a particular region

borough (BUR-oh)   English term for a town to which the king has granted the right of self-government, usually in return for an annual tax payment

bourgeois (BOOR-jwah)   French name for a middle-class city dweller

burgesses, burghers   English names for city dwellers, especially those who own property in a borough, pay part of the borough's annual tax to the king, and enjoy special privileges and full political rights in the borough

cathedral   a church from which a bishop presides

cauldron   a large kettle

clerk   a priest or, as in *The Canterbury Tales*, a scholar studying for the priesthood

commune   a group of leading citizens bound together by oath to run their businesses and govern their city without interference from an overlord; in general, a self-governing city

convent   a group of women, called nuns, who live together and devote themselves to prayer and work; also, the building where the nuns live

founder   a craftsperson who makes metal objects by melting the metal and pouring it into molds

garderobe (GAR-drohb)   an alcove with a kind of toilet seat built over a chute or drainpipe that led to a pit in the house's cellar or to a nearby canal, stream, or ditch

guild (GILD)   an organization of people in the same craft or trade. The guild set standards of training and workmanship and looked after its members' interests in various ways

haberdasher   a merchant dealing in small goods

Islam   the religion established in the Middle East by Muhammad in the early seventh century; the Islamic name for God is Allah, and

Muhammad is revered as his prophet; followers of Islam are called Muslims

manuscript a book that is written out, illustrated, and bound by hand

mason a skilled worker who cut stone into the right shapes for building or actually constructed the stone walls of a building

monastery a community of men who devote themselves to prayer, study, and work; also, the buildings that house such a community

notary a person who wrote out legal or official documents for individuals. Like a modern notary public, a medieval notary could also certify documents to make them official.

pilgrimage a journey to an important religious site; for example, a church that houses the remains of a saint

saint a person recognized by the Church as being especially holy and able to perform miracles both in life and after death

serf an unfree peasant, with specific financial and labor obligations to an overlord

shrine a place where people pray to one particular saint or other religious figure

trestle table a table made by laying a large board across two or more supports

trivet a metal stand used under a hot dish at table

vassal a noble who holds land from a king or more powerful noble in exchange for military service and a pledge of loyalty

FOR FURTHER READING

Clare, John D., ed. *Fourteenth-Century Towns*. San Diego, New York, and London: Harcourt Brace, 1993.

Corrain, Lucia. *Giotto and Medieval Art: The Lives and Works of the Medieval Artists*. New York: Peter Bedrick Books, 1995.

Cosman, Madeleine Pelner. *Medieval Holidays and Festivals: A Calendar of Celebrations*. New York: Charles Scribner's Sons, 1981.

Hartman, Gertrude. *Medieval Days and Ways*. New York: Macmillan, 1952.

Hinds, Kathryn. *The Vikings*. New York: Marshall Cavendish, 1998.

Howarth, Sarah. *Medieval Places*. Brookfield, Conn.: Millbrook Press, 1992.

Howarth, Sarah. *What Do We Know about the Middle Ages?* New York: Peter Bedrick, 1995.

Hull, Mary. *The Travels of Marco Polo*. San Diego: Lucent Books, 1995.

Kerr, Daisy. *Medieval Town*. New York: Franklin Watts, 1997.

Langley, Andrew. *Medieval Life*. New York: Knopf, 1996.

Macauley, David. *Cathedral: The Story of Its Construction*. Boston: Houghton Mifflin, 1973.

Macdonald, Fiona. *First Facts about the Middle Ages*. New York: Peter Bedrick Books, 1997.

Macdonald, Fiona. *A Medieval Cathedral*. New York: Peter Bedrick Books, 1991.

Nardo, Don. *Life on a Medieval Pilgrimage*. San Diego: Lucent Books, 1996.

Osborne, Mary Pope. *Favorite Medieval Tales*. New York: Scholastic Press, 1998.

ON-LINE INFORMATION*

Carcassonne, Medieval Walled City.
    [http://www.europe-france.com/carcassonne/en/].
City of York Walls Tour: A Virtual Walk on York's City Walls.
    [http://www.york.gov.uk/walls/index.html].
Milot, Marie-Christine. *Paris at the Time of Philippe-Auguste.*
    [http://www.philippe-auguste.com/uk/].
Scheid, Troy, and Laura Toon. *The City of Women.*
    [http://library.advanced.org/12834/index.html].
Stones, Alison. *Images of Medieval Art and Architecture.*
    [http://info.pitt.edu/~medart/].
Widdison, Robin, et al. *Virtual Tour of Durham Cathedral.*
    [http://www.dur.ac.uk/~dla0www/c tour/cathedral.html].

*Websites change from time to time. For additional on-line information, check with the media specialist at
    your local library.

BIBLIOGRAPHY

Alsford, Stephen. *Medieval English Towns*. [http://www.trytel.com/~tristan/towns/towns.html].

Blanchard, Laura V., and Carolyn Schriber. *ORB: The Online Reference Book for Medieval Studies*. [http://orb.rhodes.edu].

Chaucer, Geoffrey. *The Canterbury Tales: A Selection*. Edited by Donald R. Howard. New York: New American Library, 1969.

Chrétien de Troyes. *Le chevalier au lion (Yvain)*. Paris: Librairie Honoré Champion, 1982.

Cosman, Madeleine Pelner. *Fabulous Feasts: Medieval Cookery and Ceremony*. New York: George Braziller, 1976.

————. *Medieval Holidays and Festivals: A Calendar of Celebrations*. New York: Charles Scribner's Sons, 1981.

Editors of Time-Life Books. *What Life Was Like in the Age of Chivalry: Medieval Europe AD 800–1500*. Alexandria, Va.: Time-Life Books, 1997.

Gies, Frances, and Joseph Gies. *Cathedral, Forge, and Waterwheel: Technology and Invention in the Middle Ages*. New York: HarperCollins, 1994.

————. *Life in a Medieval City*. New York: Harper Perennial, 1969.

————. *Women in the Middle Ages*. New York: Barnes & Noble, 1978.

Halsall, Paul, ed. *Internet Medieval Sourcebook*. [http://www.fordham.edu/halsall/sbook1.html].

Harbin, Beau A. C. NetSERF: *The Internet Connection for Medieval Resources*. [http://netserf.cua.edu/#Top].

Heer, Friedrich. Translated by Janet Sondheimer. *The Medieval World: Europe 1100–1350*. Cleveland and New York: World Publishing, 1962.

Herlihy, David, ed. *Medieval Culture and Society*. New York: Walker, 1968.

Herlihy, David. *Women, Family, and Society in Medieval Europe: Historical Essays, 1978–1991*. Providence, R.I., and Oxford, England: Berghahn Books, 1995.

Hinds, Kathryn. *Venice and Its Merchant Empire*. Unpublished manuscript, 1997.

Hoppin, Richard H. *Medieval Music*. New York: Norton, 1978.

Irvine, Martin, and Deborah Everhart. *The Labyrinth: Resources for Medieval Studies.* [http://www.georgetown.edu/labyrinth].

Luria, Maxwell S., and Richard L. Hoffman. *Middle English Lyrics.* New York and London: Norton, 1974.

Matterer, James L. *A Boke of Gode Cookery.* [http://www.godecookery.com /godeboke/godeboke.htm].

Milot, Marie-Christine. *Paris sous Philippe Auguste.* [http://www.philippe-auguste.com/].

Packard, Sidney R. *12th Century Europe: An Interpretive Essay.* Amherst: University of Massachusetts Press, 1973.

Redon, Odile, Françoise Sabban, and Silvano Serventi. Translated by Edward Schneider. *The Medieval Kitchen: Recipes from France and Italy.* Chicago: University of Chicago Press, 1998.

Shahar, Shulamith. Translated by Chaya Galai. The Fourth Estate: A History of Women in the Middle Ages. London and New York: Methuen, 1983.

INDEX

Page numbers for illustrations are in boldface